BEWARE THE EXPLODING YOGHURT POT

HEATHER COOK
DRAWINGS BY HEATHER MOULSON

First Published in Great Britain by Crystal Clear Books 2025

Copyright © Heather Cook and Heather Moulson, 2025

Heather Cook has asserted her moral right under the Copyright Design and Patents Act 1988 to be identified as the author of this work.

This book is a work of poetry and, except in the case of historical fact, any resemblance to actual persons, living or dead, is purely coincidental.

No paragraph of this publication may be reproduced, copied, stored or transmitted in any format save with written permission or in accordance with the provisions of the Copyright, Designs and Patents Act 1988, or under the terms of any license, permitting limited copying issued by the Copyright Licensing Agency, 33 Alfred Place, London, WC1E 7DP.

No part of this book may be used in any manner in the learning, training or development of generative artificial intelligence technologies (including but not limited to machine learning models and large language models whether by data scraping, data mining or use in any way to create or form a part of data sets or in any other way.

Published by: Crystal Clear Books: www.crystalclearbooks.co.uk

ISBN: 978-1-0684474-3-3

Cover Image: vectorpocket / Freepik

FOR ROGER

Acknowledgements

First, thank you to all the wonderful staff in the Jasmine Suite, Ashford Hospital and the Royal Surrey Cancer Centre, not only for your incredible professionalism, but for your unfailing kindness, which mattered so very much on those darker days.

My grateful thanks too to the lovely volunteers in the Fountain Centre at the Royal Surrey, who made hair loss seem like an everyday thing and were always there to support and encourage.

Thanks are also due to my friends in Woking Writers' Circle and Write Out Loud for your hugely valued support and friendship which kept me in touch with things. You are an inspiration in every way.

I am extremely grateful to my editor, Sue, who provided insight and expertise as well as some greatly valued humour along the way, and to Linda, for her unfailing patience with my nervousness around computers and for her generous encouragement, without which my Yogurt Pot might never have seen the light of day.

And to all those who visited and made me laugh throughout my deeply unattractive chemo phase – how can I possibly thank you? For all the emails, texts, delicious meals, cards, flowers, the special creams for skin that threatened to audition for a horror film, the treats that slipped down just as I thought I'd never eat again – I thank you from the bottom of my heart.

Thanks are very definitely due to my husband, Roger, who travelled with me down a road riddled with potholes, sharing the worries, driving me to endless appointments and waiting for hours in a range of hospital car parks for the lippy old bag to emerge, no doubt bearing an uncanny resemblance to a clammy mushroom. And how could I avoid paying tribute to our two cats, Stumpy Malone and Princess Lola, who kept us both diverted by making it clear that their needs must have total priority at all times.

Heather Cook

Contents

Author's Note 1
Beware The Exploding Yogurt Pot 3
Shock And Rage 5
    The Confessional 7
    GP Appointment 9
    Waiting 10
    Hospital Appointment 11
    Diagnosis – Appointment With The Consultant 13
    This Pleasant Lady 15
    Cancer Wolf 16
    Telling People 17
    Feral Woman 18
    Don't Call It A Pathway 19
    Make Me Angry 20
Preparation 21
    The Scan 23
    Hospital Gowns 25
    Unworthy Breasts 29
Acceptance 31
    Greet Your Chemo With A Smile 33
    Brain Turned To Mush 34
    Sinead O'Connor 36
    Lucozade 37
    Loneliness In Bay 3 39
    Cravings 41
    Hats 45
    A Taste Of Honey 46
    Unfledged At Chemo Treatment No 4 47
Trudging Down The Pathway 49
    The Beech And I 51
    Shopping Spree 52
    It's Done 53

Author's Note

Beware the Exploding Yogurt Pot is my personal account of being diagnosed with breast cancer in my 70s and how I felt and dealt with the experience.

Being told I'd got cancer and going through chemo, scans and various associated and fairly unpleasant procedures brought me face-to-face with the lippy old bag that is, apparently, the real me.

The content of this pamphlet breaks every rule that I have ever tried to follow as a writer and particularly as a poet. The poems and observations are raw, rude and real.

Heather Cook

Beware The Exploding Yogurt Pot

So full of fruity innocence,
it sits there on the shelf,
promising a tranquil gut
and blooming inner health.

You ladle it on strawberries
with a generous swirl of honey,
relishing its creaminess,
its taste so clean and sunny.

But beware the maverick yogurt pot
that without a rhyme or reason
explodes and coats your gleaming fridge:
an act of bacterial treason.

I've always thought of yoghurt as a fairly unexciting but enjoyable commodity that sits patiently in the fridge waiting to be useful. It is generally thought of as being a 'good thing', until it explodes. And that unfortunate episode is exactly what I thought of when cancer suddenly threatened my very contented life in the summer of 2024.

Shock And Rage

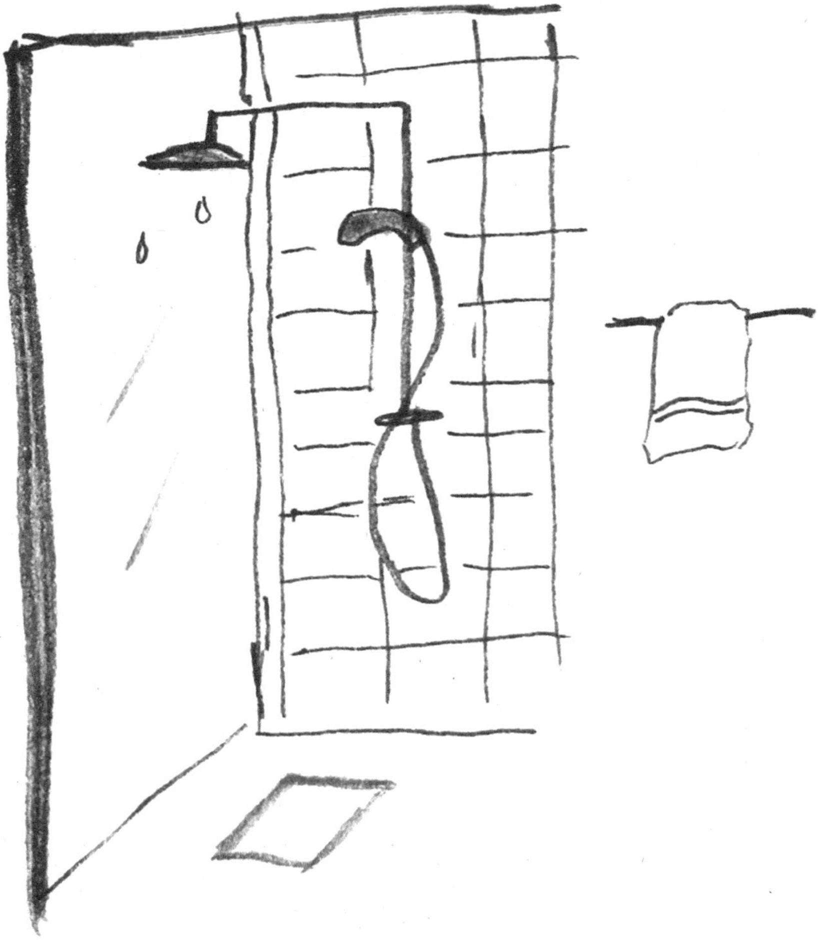

The Confessional

The clammy curtains
of the walk-in shower
have always sheltered secrets.

This is where I shave the places
that I rarely see,
bend awkwardly to wash
arthritic toes.

Now a new secret
condenses round me,
circling the drain,
but doesn't flush away.

I hold my arm
in different poses
so the lump seems smaller.
It's probably a sprain.

Gardening could do it.
It doesn't hurt.
A nagging voice tells me
it would be better if it did.

GP Appointment

I thought I might ignore it,
my unnamed secret,
but the cloud I dodged beneath
is hogging all the light.

I'm in the GP's waiting room,
made brave by fear.

I hone a jokey speech for friends,
about the doctor telling me it's nothing.
"Drama Queen," they'll say.
We'll pour another drink.

Someone scrapes the car on my way home.
I'm almost glad.

I've come to realise the significance and often positive value of distractions when something really worrying is on the agenda. Obsessed with the possibility of a positive cancer diagnosis, the scrape on the car was helpful, but later on something more dramatic was needed to divert me through the weary days of waiting – first for the diagnosis and then while waiting for the results of other tests to see if tumours existed elsewhere in the body. Be careful what you wish for! A sickening fall in the garden delivered the goods in the form of a broken ankle. Not that I thought it was broken, of course, and tottered around on it for several days before an x-ray confirmed a fracture.

It was the breast unit consultant who referred me for the x-ray, the result being that I had a positive diagnosis of cancer and confirmation that the ankle was broken within an hour.

WAITING

The days cannot help their passing.
Sometimes they slow, or gather speed,
just when I think
I could hide in Thursday afternoon forever
and never hear the news that waits
the other side of now.

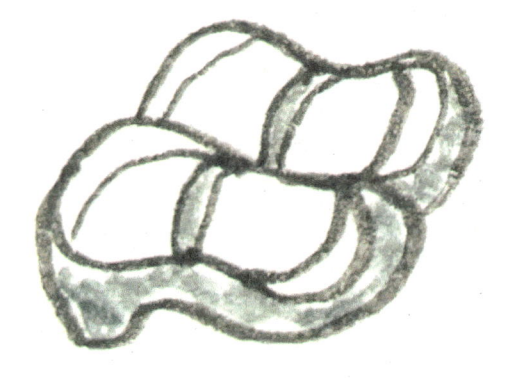

Hospital Appointment

My old black cat
turns panther on the sill,
young and sinuous
in dawn's uncertain light.

I've slept somehow,
sleep filled with cameos:
my laughing doctor
putting colour on my hair,
joking semi-permanent will do;
Christmas cards
with the 'and' after my partner's name
trailing downwards, unlinked, unheld;
fridge shelves groaning
with pork pies.

I'll know this afternoon.
Is it decided?
Or if I wear my lucky shoes,
might it be different?

Diagnosis – Appointment With The Consultant

Finally, the word pops out
after undue consideration
of the weather and the traffic situation.

A breath-sucking balloon winds me,
erasing features, stealing who I am.
I swear and cannot stop.

After years of deathly silence
I hear my mother's voice.
Of course, far worse than having cancer
would be to make a silly fuss.

I make an effort. Thank the powerful one,
try to grasp what happens next.
He's shuffling papers, moving on.

Osmosis moves me to a room
of drooping posters, thank you cards,
messy racks of photocopied leaflets.

A glass of water. My time is up.
Nurse tells me parking will be free.

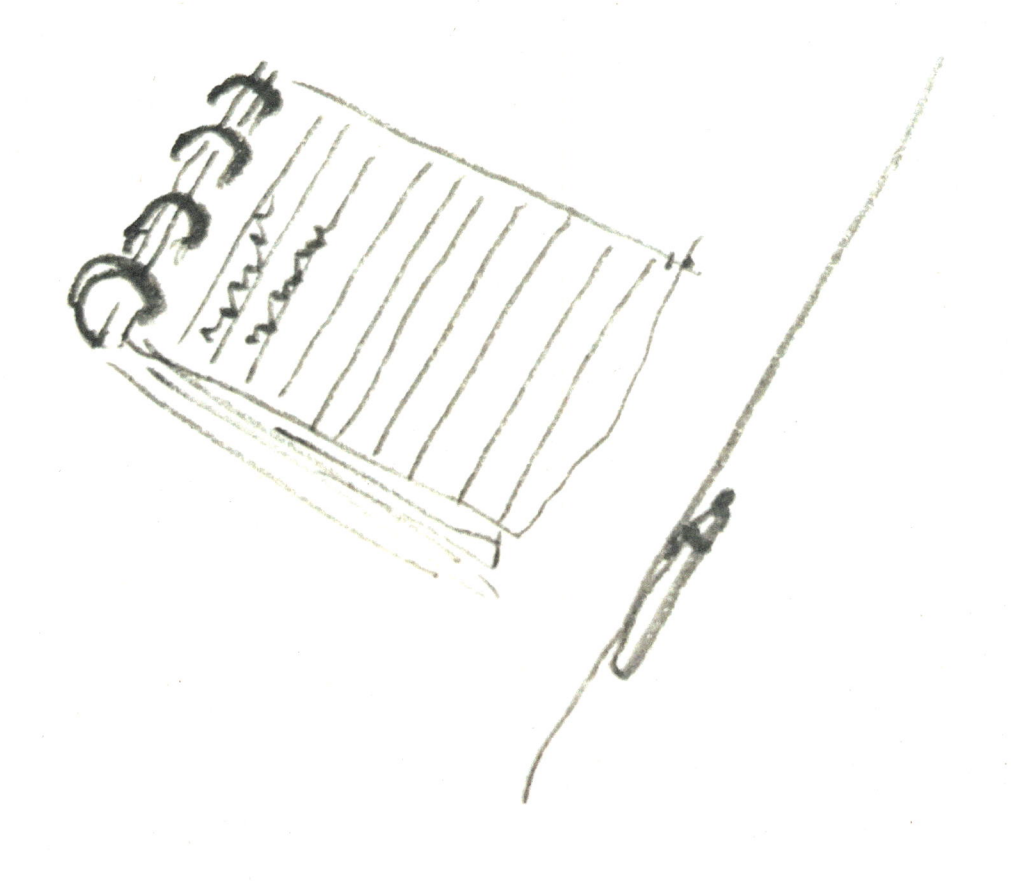

This Pleasant Lady

I have a copy of the diagnosis letter
from the powerful one
to a GP I've never met.

He is so grateful to him or her
for referring 'this pleasant lady'
to his clinic.

I snigger at the 'pleasant'.
Does this mean I didn't smell or spit,
or is it code for 'thanks for nothing',

this 'pleasant' woman is a lippy bag
who wields a notebook
like a gun?

Cancer Wolf

Forget the distorted shadow
ripping at a carcass,
pulling shadows round him
like a shroud.

The cancer wolf
sees no need to slink.
He struts and skips
down well-lit ways,
pulls up a chair,
peers into faces,
marks them with a cross.

He serves the Lord of Averages,
seeks out the one in three,
the two point five,
whatever is the target for the day.

I don't always think of cancer as a wolf. More frequently, I visualise a caterpillar, a soft, creeping creature that feeds off me before it turns into a chrysalis - a hard lump of nastiness. Even the words 'cancer' and 'caterpillar' have a similar shape – sinuous and sneaky. Butterflies are beautiful, of course, but all that fluttering could be dangerous in terms of spreading the evilness of cancer round the body.

I was fortunate. The PET scan given before treatment started could find no trace of cancer in any other part of my body, so the poor old right boob was the lucky location of my problem, with comradely support from the lymph nodes under my right arm.

And yes, I know this is common and I know it could have been so much worse. In some ways, it was even quite interesting. But I sincerely hope I never have to repeat the experience.

TELLING PEOPLE

It's so important not to boast
or think you're something special
and assume the role of martyr
as if cancer's made you better,
more sensitive and worthy
because you've stopped the bullet
that would have felled another
if you had tried to duck it.

And it's not a competition,
so don't try to trump a rash
with details of your chemo –
that's just common, rude and brash.

You must try hard not to languish
or be ages in the loo
because the kindest, oldest friends
could soon grow tired of you.

Feral Woman

It's late in life
to meet my feral self again.

To feel the anger
of the girl
who marched against the bomb,
who shook her parents'
cautious post-war lives
with pink hair, cheap booze
and late, late nights.

The layered niceties
have vanished overnight,
unsupported by wise Nature's
evolutionary plod.

Why wouldn't I be wild?
The shadows
of the sabre-tooth and wolf
that stalked my kin
still lurk in Waitrose' car park.

Don't Call It A Pathway

I cannot think of it that way,
however much you smile
and say my name.
It is a tunnel.

There may be glimpses
of the light;
pinpricks of brightness
where the roof leaks hope.
I doubt it though,
even as I clasp
the catalogue of wigs
and list of therapies.

A pathway would be lined
with mossy banks,
home to tiny scuttling things,
lit with toadflax, foxgloves, ferns.
The overarching trees
would filter dancing light.
Not bury me in darkness.

Make Me Angry

                                      make me angry

make me bald

        make sure I don't do

                                what I'm told

          never mind

                                    how rough it gets

                let me keep

my feral soul

At one early meeting with the oncologist, he was telling me about the nature of the tumour in my right breast. 'Small and aggressive' was how he described it. For a moment I thought he was referring to me.

PREPARATION

THE SCAN

My body spreads across the slab
beneath a roof that's full of
lights and clicks.

I gulp and hold my breath
as if there will never be
more air.

Flesh still wobbles
to and fro or
round and round;

I cannot tell.

My eyes are closed;
I'm lost, then calm
as tickling probes invade
the sticky darkness, criss-crossed
by Central lines of radioactive dye.
I let my secrets go.

I let my secrets go,
releasing them from fleshy folds.
All boundaries dissolve
between soft thought, hard bone.

Let the watchers see them,
make of them what they will.
No choice remains,
just unsought comfort
in this petite mort.

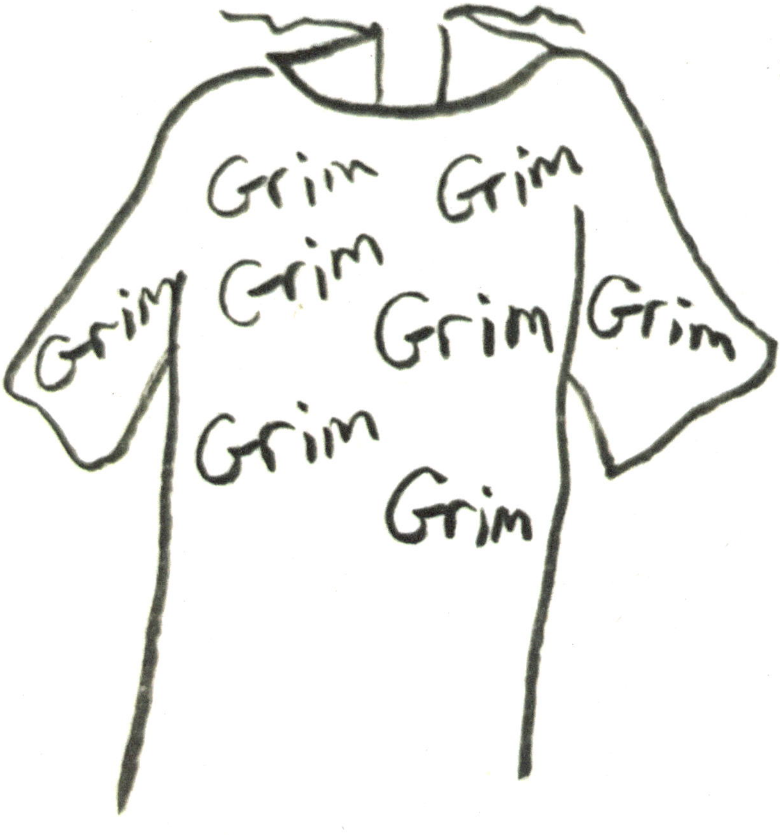
Grim
Grim
Grim
Grim
Grim
Grim
Grim
Grim

Hospital Gowns

These prickly pornographic rags
cut skin already bruised,
pull stitches,
gape revealingly
and won't soak up
the very smallest bead of sweat.

They conspire with clinging curtains
to humiliate the damaged breast
that has been seen,
probed and marked
by everybody present.

Why can't I stand before you,
nurses, doctors,
nobly naked?
It is these writhing antics
that steal my dignity,
induce false shame
and make of me a victim.

The Power Of The Notebook

It's a feature of professionals
to adopt a lofty pose
when addressing clients
who no doubt they suppose

will struggle with the content
of their learned exposition,
dwelling in a murky world
of soaps and superstition.

My consultant is a pleasant man,
smiling and urbane.
He said too much and far too fast
and all behind his hand.

I took my notebook from my bag
and lodged it on my knee;
he didn't seem to like it much
which mattered not to me.

I needed to be clear about
the treatment he had planned
and while he was explaining,
please would he move his hand?

A Small Procedure

It was, of course, a small procedure. The fitting of a portacath – a handy thing to be inserted under skin, joined to a vein, to facilitate the unimpeded flow of poison. My high blood pressure, generated by my unnatural level of anxiety was a mystery and an inconvenience, necessitating liberal doses of expensive sedative. Who wouldn't be anxious, I protested, pinned down on a slab beneath a plastic sheet with a bloke almost on top of me scratching lesions in my skin?

I recovered quickly and was wedging down restorative portions of lasagne at home when I felt a warm trickling sensation on my left side, a sensation promoted to fully-fledged alarm when I saw what looked like quite a lot of blood running down my arm. By that time, the only place to take my panic was A&E, where hope was raised by being seen within minutes of arrival. This proved to be a cruel trick; after questioning and inspection of my soggy dressing I was told to return to my seat.

Unrecognisable names were called to deaf, anxious and exhausted patients from various directions. The process of following the fleeting figure was rendered trickier by the determination of man with a cleaning trolley to impede the tottering steps of anyone struggling to reach a given point.

There was a great deal of flesh and blood, the latter generally being mopped up by anxious companions with filthy sodden tissues. Very few people appeared to be fully dressed, by which I don't mean they were in pyjamas, just that they appeared to be wearing particularly skimpy underclothes or beachwear. Not that I'm one to judge. I just felt ridiculously overdressed in t-shirt and jeans at 11pm.

The shock of being called was overwhelming, but I soon realised this was not the beginning of the end, nor was it the end of the beginning. I had a whole clutch of excitements, including x-rays, blood tests and an ECG. Thankfully the bleeding had stopped or a blood transfusion would have been another treat.

Entertainment stepped up a level as midnight came and went, with various men being brought in by Police escorts. The escorted men were the life and soul of the place, seeming to know every nurse and doctor who sloped into view. In sad contrast children pale with tiredness were carried about by hollow-eyed parents, swathed in blankets and often clutching well-sucked teddies in tiny dirty hands.

Soon after 1am, I was told that I wasn't bleeding to death and would be free to go after the dressings had been changed.

Never before had the polluted car park air seemed so sweet.

Unworthy Breasts

Mine are unworthy breasts.
They have succoured no babes,
rested no troubled childish heads
against their pillowed warmth.

They are frivolous, teasing breasts;
or were.
Now they are marked, diminished,
scarred with metal markers, stitched,
bruised by cold professional hands
with cold, professional aims.

Worthy breasts would still be beautiful,
still be revered for past labours.
Their scars would be caressed,
awarded Madonna status.

ACCEPTANCE

GREET YOUR CHEMO WITH A SMILE

A lymph node is a lovely thing
that gobbles up infection
until it gets invaded,
takes a sinister direction.

It has a sharing nature
so struggles to refrain
from sending cancer cells to play
in livers, kidneys, brains.

So greet your chemo with a smile,
applaud the loss of hair;
if you don't, it's true to say
you'll not be here to care.

Brain Turned To Mush

I wander round my head
searching for a name.

The version of myself
that stalks this inner world
can hardly move today.

A small hope flutters in the hands
that reach towards the cupboard
where the teabags are.
I think the name I'm searching for
might be in there too.

September Leaf Fall

Why wouldn't hair fall out
in seasonal sympathy
with those first floating leaves
that drift to earth without regret?

I was expecting it. Had been told,
but seeing that white basin
darkened by my carefully coloured locks
was still a bloody awful shock.

Sinead O'Connor

I think a lot about that perfect head,
the glory of those sculpted lines.
Hair could only dull that shining orb,
reduce it to an ordinary beauty.

Bald with sparse and barely coloured strands,
my head resembles a misshapen globe,
a swollen pale celeriac root,
as far from that ideal as it could be.

Lucozade

Chemo's made a child of me
with a fancy for Lucozade,
that startling orange drink
that takes me back to days off school,
spent wrapped in scratchy blankets.
My mother blamed illicit sweets.
No one ever thought of stress,
except in engineering terms.

Weakened now by health-restoring poison,
I greet my orange chum once more,
relieved to find him snazzily repackaged
with a host of sporty friends.

Dressing For Chemo

Elastic-waisted trousers
and a generous baggy top
that facilitate a fiddle
to connect me up,

that's my uniform for chemo,
undemanding, never tight,
with scope for spit and spillage,
keeping secrets out of sight,

unlike the woman in the corner,
who is firmly in control,
tapping briskly at her laptop
while poison claims her soul.

LONELINESS IN BAY 3

His wife smiles broadly.
He'll be here for the day,
but the bags she's carrying
would equip an expedition.

He falls asleep while she's still waving,
then speaks so suddenly, I jump.

We chat.
His cancer's terminal.
Six months at the most.

I say the obvious things:
how hard, how difficult for family.

He says they can't accept he's dying.
He's doing chemo just for them,
when all he wants to do is die.

He's lonely now in these last days,
silenced by their love.

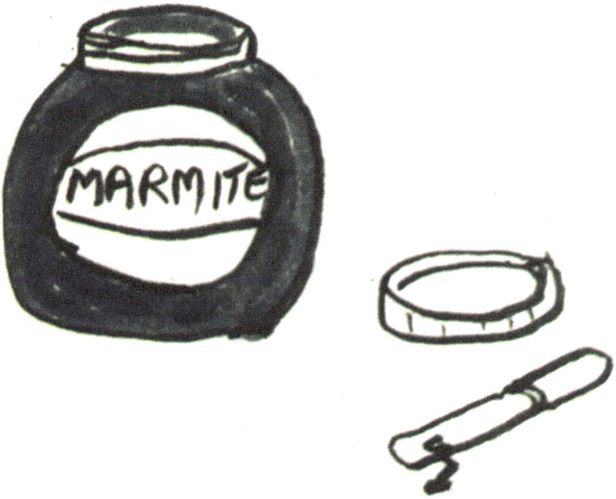
MARMITE

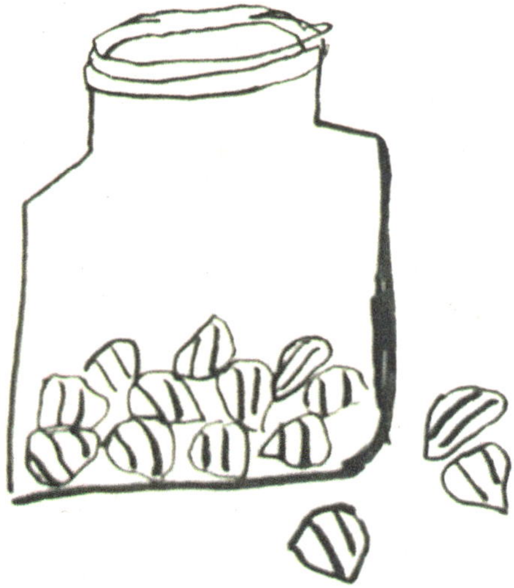

CRAVINGS

It's a feature, I've been told,
the chemo mouth that tastes like lead.
I reach for wine, withdraw my hand
and pour an apple juice instead.
Coffee, my habitual fix,
before I face the brightening day,
smells like rancid fish oil now;
I turn away, I turn away.

It's strange the things I crave today
that were strangers to my trolley.
Marmite, garlic, crisp pak choi
make my suppers almost jolly.
And late at night I must have sweetness –
ice-cream, a sugary lump of pie.
It's lucky I'm not diabetic;
'not yet, not yet!' you cry.

When Am I?

Waking in my chair,
I look out on a garden
full of gentle light.

When am I? Dawn or dusk?
I'm in my chair, cat on lap,
but have I lost a day?

'When' comes slowly into view,
pulling on its shoes,
wondering where it left its specs.

Coping

Different people,
different ways of coping.

I favour rage. Purging and unreasonable,
it cleanses this invaded body.

My partner copes by filling up the fridge
with food that fed his bachelor days.

Solid pies weigh down the shelves:
Melton Mowbray, steak and ale. Rarely fish.

He seeks the life he had before the Age of Veg,
when green leaves cluttered up his plate;

he longs for simpler times before
I lured him to this world of complications.

Pies are his comfort. Can I resist the urge
to fling them to the foxes?

As a retired couple, we're used to spending time together, but there is a huge difference in time spent together doing things and socialising and time spent when one of you is not feeling well. Diary entries for all sorts of jolly things were soon replaced with crossings out and medical appointments. The number of blood tests, minor procedures and conversations with consultants that had to be ticked off before the planned treatment could begin was mind boggling.

 At an early stage, I was able to take the indulgent decision that I would leave the driving to Roger, which was a huge relief as my concentration (never a strong point) took a holiday. We didn't always take the same view of the success or otherwise of a particular hospital trip. An example was when we returned home from one morning appointment.

'Well,' said Roger complacently, 'I thought this morning went really well.'

I smiled wanly, knowing I would return to the subject more spiritedly later. 'It was quite unpleasant, having that metal marker coil inserted.'

Hats

My school hat was a fearful thing –
a navy pudding basin
that no young girl would willingly
deign to show her face in.

But time's a marvellous healer
and I'm bald as a bloater,
always combing charity shops
for a trilby or a boater.

And should my hair decide to sprout
(you can place your bets on that one)
it will have stiff competition
from a rather fetching stetson.

A Taste Of Honey

I'm pretty certain I'm not pregnant,
but these cravings are insistent;
my desire for cheese and Marmite
is both alarming and persistent.

Those tooth-decaying humbugs
are like a drug these days,
gluing jaws together
while I dribble, snore and laze.

I no longer slurp a Merlot
while I'm preparing dinner;
the sight of that dark bottle
leaves me shivering like a swimmer.

The raspberries I'd have killed for
seem pippy and acidic,
while strawberries laced with honey
taste like an aphrodisiac.

Sadly, it's not healthy leaves
that will help me beat this,
but Marmite and an endless trail
of gloopy, honeyed sweetness.

Unfledged At Chemo Treatment No 4

The unfledged chick
that's fallen from the nest
seeks shelter
from the treacherous light.

I flap towards the green familiar chair,
settle, fluffed and fearful,
low down in the seat,
clutching the pillow
to still my fluttering.

I seek out faces seen before,
encouraged by a smile,
a conspiratorial shrug.

As poison drips into my veins,
I find I'm listening for the tea trolley.
Custard creams would hit the spot.

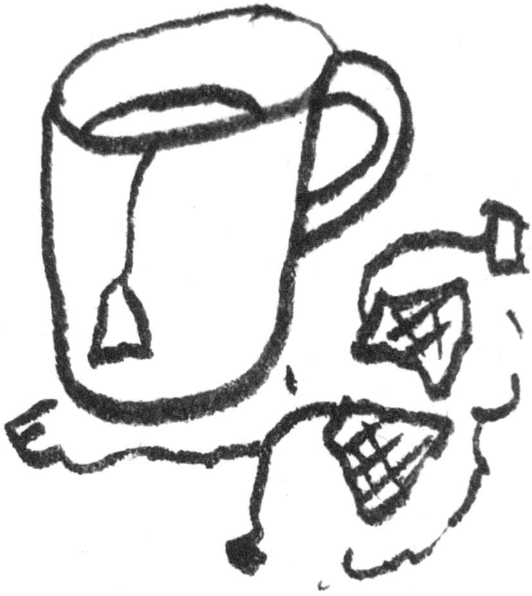

Trudging Down The Pathway

It is 5th December and I have one more scheduled chemo treatment. The last two treatments have really challenged this old body. I seem to have ticked every box in the long list of side effects, including nose bleeds, joint pains, loss of appetite, neuropathy and a particularly unpleasant and persistently itchy rash.

I have the final chemotherapy treatment a week before Christmas, but am so weary that instead of celebrating, I snooze and dribble in my chair for hours on end. In the New Year there will be discussion about the next steps, the most likely one being an operation to remove what's left of the tumour in the right breast and the lymph nodes under my right arm. There will be radiotherapy and scans – and chats between a totally reasonable consultant and a lippy, bald old bag.

The Beech And I

I have been watching
for those first few precious shoots,
the greening of the stark, pollarded twigs
against a blur of woodland.

I have been feeling
for those first few stubbly hairs
to pierce my shiny scalp,
rasp against these bright tied scarves.

The greening rises to the light
as days quite suddenly lengthen.
The ancient beech needs leaves to live,
my hair is merely vanity.

I have always felt close to the beech. This splendid old tree at the bottom of my garden was the main reason I moved here and when it was badly damaged by the Great Storm in 1987, I shrugged off advice to have it felled. It was pinned, trimmed, its height reduced and every spring I have watched anxiously for those first green shoots to appear. Witnessing its re-birth this year was an unashamedly emotional experience.

SHOPPING SPREE

The operation's days away,
So I'm busy on-line shopping
To buy front-opening nighties
And a bra to restrict flopping.

Day surgery, then home I'll come
To doze and snort and dribble,
Fending off a clingy cat
While I attempt to nibble

Scrambled egg on Hovis toast
And sip a weak, sweet tea.
But that's to come in 4 days' time –
Today's a shopping spree.

It's Done

The operation's done,
I'm home by half past three.
I wish that I could bottle this relief.

I feel no pain,
but soon the waiting will begin.
Biopsies keep no secrets.

Stray rogue cells could mean more treatment,

But for now, relief is all I want to feel.

I believe the worst is over. I also believe that there will be lots of waiting both now and in future, and that I shall have to grow used to this way of living.

I am extremely fortunate – to benefit from the huge medical advances made in the past few years and to have what is hopefully a fairly treatable, if locally aggressive, form of cancer.

My experiences have been humbling. The bravery of fellow patients has made me conscious of my own wobbliness. I have been overwhelmed by the kindness of friends and the professionals administering the various treatments. Kindness, above all things, has brought such comfort, even in my darkest moments.

I am closing the door on cancer now, although there is every possibility that it will not be closing the door on me. I am eager to move forward, to ease back into normality, while remembering how very privileged I am to be alive.